Rat

Horoscope 2023

By
IChingHun FengShuisu

Table of Contents

Introduce

The character of people born in the year of the rat

Rats prefer to live in packs. You have a large community as a result of your habitual politeness. There are numerous connections. On the other hand, allowing anyone to enter into a deep relationship with each other is extremely rare. You appear to be a patient individual who is unconcerned about the end of the world. But you're nervous because of the relaxed atmosphere. You value your solitude and privacy. Anyone who enters your life uninvitedly will be dizzy from your sharp lips. Rats are self-centered, stubborn creatures who prefer to solve problems on their own. Personal transactions where no one will threaten or cause problems. Parents who enjoy playing with their children are known as rat parents.

People born in this year are typically smart, intelligent, and capable of surviving. Beliefs of the ancient Chinese If there are mice in the house, it is believed that food will be plentiful throughout the year.

Strength:
Rat people have a high level of intelligence. It also conceals the habit of cheating and preferring to socialize first. People born in this year are frequently successful entrepreneurs.

Weaknesses:
As a result of being overly ambitious, frequently leads to mistakes.

Love:
People born this year have less romantic love as a result of a mischievous child's personality. People born in this year, on the other hand, simply love someone who adores and despise someone who worships. As a result, those who want to break the heart of someone born this year should reconsider their urgent plan. People born in this year are lovely. However, the love of the year is not always long-lasting. We have a simple love habit. The habit is not stubborn, prefers consistency, and is frequently obsessed with eroticism.

Suitable Career:

People born in the year of the rat are classified as belonging to the water element. Opening a store, selling liquor, beer, and seafood, opening a shipping company, building a boat, developing a tour company, a diplomat, an accountant, a finance company, a salesman, a broker, a negotiating job, a job related to the sale of metal and jewelry, selling jewelry or machinery, etc. are all appropriate occupations for those born in the year of the rat.

Year of the Rat (Fire) | (1936) & (1996)

"The Rat in the Barn" is a person born in the year of the Rat at the age of 87 years (1936) and 27 years (1996)

Overview

Although the planet orbiting this year is Tianik, the fate of about 87 years old is mysterious. However, because the year of birth coincides with the sign "Buoy," it is considered a bad year, particularly for conflicts and the loss of family property. However, it is fortunate that in destiny, there is still a star Tian Yik to assist. The story remains positive, and you will receive encouragement from those around you. However, this year you should make merit, make merit, and ask the gods for blessings. It will aid in disaster protection and mitigation. Because there are important health issues that you should be aware of, especially during the 2nd month of China (6 Mar. – 4 Apr.), the 6th month of China (7 Jul. – 7 Aug.), and the 8th month of China (8 Sept. – 7/Oct.) Be careful of relapses and other hidden diseases Asked for this year should be monitored for abnormalities in the body. And always rushing to see a doctor for health checks will help lighten the burden.

Career and Business

Even this year, the job duties or trade for which you are accountable. Moving forward will be difficult and burdensome. However, in a challenging environment, you and your colleagues must plan carefully. Set clear objectives and goals. To overcome it, both must move forward. Otherwise, it will lag and fall behind. Maintaining a good relationship with the people around you at both the upper and lower levels, including customers and people who must be in constant contact, will help you resolve well this year. During the month that the job declines and encounters obstacles, the following issues arise: 2nd month of China (6 Mar. - 4 Apr.), 5th month of China (6 Jun. - 6 Jul.), 6th month of China (7 Jul. – 7 Aug.) and the 8th month of China (8 Sep. – 7 Oct.) Be wary of accepting work; poor communication will harm you, and avoid interpersonal conflicts. The month in which various investment projects will prosper, including the 12th month of China (5 Jan. – 3 Feb.), the 3rd month of China (5 Apr. – 5 May), the 7th month of China (8 Aug. – 7 Sep.) and the 11th month of China (7 Dec 23 – 5 Jan 24)

Financial
This year's financial horoscope has been risky. As a result, capital management is extremely challenging. Because unexpected events frequently have an impact, you should manage your capital and invest under your authority.

Overdrafts and long-term debt obligations pose greater risks than smooth sailing. As a result, you should not underestimate the importance of financial management and should keep a close eye on it. I request that you save anything that can be saved first. Don't be self-centered by agreeing to sign a guarantee for someone else. You'll be in big trouble if you don't. Especially during the months when the financial stumble, such as the 2nd month of China (6 Mar. – 4 Apr.), the 5th month of China (6 Jun. – 6 Jul.), the 6th month of China (7 Jul. – 7 Aug.) and the 8th month of China (8 Sep. – 7 Oct.). Do not conduct any business that is insulting the law. And should avoid gambling and gamble to maintain liquidity in the system. As for the months that your finances have good liquidity, they are: 12th month of China (5 Jan. – 3 Feb.), 3rd month of China (5 Apr. – 5 May), 7th month of China (8 Aug. – 7 Sep.) and 11th month China (7 Dec. 23 – 5 Jan. 24)

Family

This year, the family horoscope has auspicious power to visit. You have the opportunity to host a variety of auspicious events in your home.

There may be betrothal, marriage, marriage, and marriage, or there may be repairs or house merits. However, if the family enters the following month, they will encounter chaos, including 2nd month of China (6 Mar. – 4 Apr.), 5th month of China (6 Jun. – 6 Jul.), 6th month of China (7 Jul. - 7 Aug.) and 8th month of China (8 Sep. - 7 Oct.) to ensure the safety of children and the elderly in the home who may sustain blood injuries if the tires fall out, you should also inspect the items attached to the house. If an old, damaged piece of equipment or attachment has been attached for an extended period, it should be repaired to keep it operational. In Elder Destiny, trips and falls will result in injury or bone problems. As a result, if you feel dizzy or faint, take a seat and rest. Furthermore, the two age cycles guard against thieves.

Love

In support of Elder Destiny, the fact that you do not interfere with children's matters even though there are many children in the house will enable you to be loved and respected as before. As for young people, especially young women, who do not have a boyfriend this year, you have the criteria to find the right person in the specifications that you are looking for. Those who have loved ones who already have a friendship report that the relationship is progressing well and that they have a good understanding of each other. There is a requirement for those who marry this year to have children in a golden chain. However, keep in mind that love is quite fragile during the months: 2nd month of China (6 Mar. - 4 Apr.), 5th month of China (6 Jun. - 6 Jul.), 6th month of China (7 Oct. – 7 Aug.) and the 8th month of China (8 Sept. – 7 Oct.) where you should be careful with your own words, some words may break the heart of the other person They should avoid becoming the third party in other couples' relationships and should avoid going to places of entertainment or secret places where prostitutes are sold. Because there are endless opportunities for squabbles. As a bonus, both have the potential to become infected with a disease.

Health

In both of these years, your health horoscope is not favorable. Because of the health house, evil stars have appeared to infest, causing accidents, disasters, and hidden diseases. As a result, please take care of any abnormalities that occur in the body. Both should have annual health checks regularly. This year, including local and long-distance travel, you must be cautious and prioritize the safety of you and your family. In particular, you need to be very careful during the 2nd month of China (6 Mar. – 4 Apr.), the 5th month of China (6 Jun. – 6 Jul.), the 6th month of China (7 Jul. – 7 Aug.), and the 8th month of China (8 Sept. – 7 Oct.)

Year of the Rat (Earth) | (1948) & (2008)

"The Rat in the beam" is a person born in the year of the Rat at the age of 75 years (1948) and 15 years (2008)

Overview

For the senior destiny due to the planets orbiting affecting this year's destiny, Jiang Chae and Sam Tai, All of them represent honor and rank. This year will be a breeze for you. Everything will change for the better. If you are considering doing anything, there will be people who will assist you along the way. As a result, in the workplace, you should focus on the transfer of your children. And you should find happiness in doing things you enjoy. However, because of the fate of the funeral guests, who are both maligned and harassed, this year, the fate must be cautious of health issues, particularly heart disease. Gastritis and inflammatory bowel disease unexpected events may result in injuries, bleeding, or rubber out. There is also a mourning criterion in the family. You should make time at the start of the year to pay homage to the gods and the

Tai tribute gods. to request your assistance in protecting them from various dangers.

For the teenage planet orbiting into your destiny, this year's Support Star is thus considered an auspicious year to visit this year's education as a whole as a progressive criterion. You have the opportunity to be fulfilled if you want to continue your studies or transfer to a new school. However, because there are unfortunate stars in destiny waiting to disturb and focus on them, destiny must be cautious of being persuaded by friends or gatherings to do something out of the ordinary. because your rage may lead to unanticipated adversity.

Career and Business

For the young destiny, it's because there are patronage stars and star warlords to help them. As a result, learning takes a step forward. There are some criteria that you can use if you are planning to study abroad. If you increase your diligence this year, you will receive excellent support. And as you gain more knowledge, you will be able to make much faster progress. But you should be careful not to be arrogant and set yourself up for failure, or to commit adultery. In addition to lowering, one's chances, one may be duped by those who do not wish to cause trouble. Especially during the months that will encounter obstacles, including 2nd month of China (6 Mar. – 4 Apr.), 5th month of China (6 Jun. – 6 Jul.), 6th month of China (7 Jul. - 7 Aug.), and the 8th month of China (8 Sep - 7 Oct.). The month in which the start of new jobs, education, and various investments this year will be prosperous, including the 12th month of China (5 Jan. – 3 Feb.), the 3rd month of China (5 Apr. – 5 May), 7th month of China (8 Aug. – 7 Sep.), and 11th month, China (7th Dec. 23 – 5 Jan.24)

Financial

The financial fortunes of this year's two destinies rest on their seats. Unforeseen expenses, both medical and otherwise, appear to intervene. As a result, you should take an economical approach to all activities. Purchasing expensive items should be postponed if not necessary to have more cash in your pockets. And you should plan your finances carefully at the start of the year. Don't lend money or make guarantees on behalf of others to make up for lost pocket money. Especially the months when the financial star turned down, including the 2nd month of China (6 Mar – 4 Apr), the 5th month of China (6 Jun – 6 Jul), the 6th month of China (7 Jul. – 7 Aug.) and the 8th month of China (8 Sep. – 7 Oct.) You should avoid investing in all types of risk. Neither investment nor involvement in any business that is insulting the law is prohibited. Otherwise, it will affect you and your family members even more. For the month of bright and prosperous financial fortunes, such as the 12th month of China (5 Jan. – 3 Feb.), the 3rd month of China (5 Apr. – 5th May), the 7th month of China (8 Aug. – 7 Sep.) and 11th month of China (7 Dec. 23 – 5 Jan. 24)

Family

Because funeral guests are watching, family fortunes are considered good and bad. As a result, the fate of both ages should be mindful of the health of the elderly at home. And be aware that rage will cause harm. Both age cycles will experience chaos, especially during the month in which the destiny's family is born, including the 2nd month of China (6 Mar. - 4 Apr.), the 5th month of China (6 Jun. - 6 Jul.), 6th month of China (7 Jul - 7 Aug.) and 8th month of China (8 Sep. - 7 Oct.) are the months to pay special attention to home security. Be wary of the little servants' carelessness, which will result in losses. Both will face conflicts and be wary of accidents that will result in blood loss.

Love

This year's love forecast for the two fates has been rather flat and depressing. Seniors would receive good care and respect from their grandchildren if he wasn't too much of a bother to the people around them. However, if the relationship is in danger in the coming months. Avoid collisions in the following months: 2nd month of China (6 Mar. - 4 Apr.), 5th month of China (6 Jun. - 6 Jul.), 6th month of China (7 Jul. - 7 Oct.), and 8th month of China (8 Sep. – 7 Oct.) When it comes to adolescent fate, the most prudent thing to do is to foster an environment that fosters lust and insufferable. Allowing one-on-one time in private places is the most effective way to protect teenagers. Especially during the months mentioned above, and if the other party terminates the relationship, you must restrain yourself and unconditionally love yourself, believing that heartbreak is preferable to not being able to love.

Health

This year, Senior Elders' physical health has been poor, with frequent illnesses. They must also be aware of gastritis, intestinal disease, liver disease, and old and new complications that they can request. As a result, you should be stricter about taking care of yourself, such as exercising and eating a healthy diet, as well as attending your doctor's appointments regularly. Especially during the month when fate is supposed to take care of the body's health, such as the 2nd month of China (6 Mar. - 4 Apr.), the 5th month of China (6 Jun. - 6 Jul), the 6th month of China (7 Jul. - 7 Aug.), and the 8th month of China (8 Sep. - 7 Oct.), where the senior must be cautious of illnesses that necessitate a lengthy stay. As for the adolescent's health throughout the month. Accidents from sports and other activities, such as traveling and driving vehicles, should be avoided.

Year of the Rat (Golden) | (1960)

"The Rat on the Beam of the House" is a person born in the year of the Rat at the age of 63 years (1960)

Overview

Many bad stars are focusing on and being classified as another zodiac sign "Phua" for the destiny around this age, this year, even in your destiny house, but many auspicious stars are shining to help. These include the stars "Tian Yik," "Sue Ha," and "Jiang Chae," so the fate criteria are considered to be half good and half bad. There will be progress in the direction of work and business. However, you must not be careless; you must constantly analyze and check for flaws and deficiencies in your work to improve and keep up with changes. This year, pay special attention to unexpected events, especially the safety and health of household members because there will be a chance to turn things around in the following year. However, if an auspicious event occurs in your home this year. It will aid in the fading of unfortunate events. However, if no auspicious event occurs, please be cautious not to be careless. You should make time at the start of the year to pay homage to the gods and pay respect to the gods of Tai tribute.

Career and Business

The work horoscope of destiny discovered auspicious stars to assist, resulting in work and business duties finding patrons to assist. Good interpersonal relationships and cooperation will allow you to advance and make your overall work easier. By the month that his work and trade are in a progressive direction, namely, the 12th month of China (5 Jan. - 3 Feb.), the 3rd month of China (5 Apr. - 5 May), the 7th month of China (8 Aug. - 7 Sep.) and the 11th month of China (7 Dec 22 - 5 Jan 23). However, there are some things you should be more cautious about, such as using servants or subordinates to work. You must select the best candidate for the job. Otherwise, there will be damage, forcing you to wait for interminable solutions. In particular, you should be very careful during the following months: 2nd month of Chinese (6 Mar. - 4 Apr.), 5th month of China (6 Jun. - 6 Jul.), 6th month of China (7 Jul. – 7 Aug.), and the 8th month of China (8 Sep. – 7 Oct.) In addition to signing various contract documents. Should consider carefully, be careful of hidden hoards that will cause you trouble.

Financial

Despite being one of the bad years, the fortune of the fortune-teller of the year of the rat Money and gold, on the other hand, have a consistent inflow of income, both regular and non-regular. Fate will have a channel to become a broker or has suggested selling the tiger with bare hands to get a large sum of money. Particularly during the fiscal month.

Especially during the very financial month, such as the 12th month of China (5 Jan. – 3 Feb.), the 3rd month of China (5 Apr. – 5 May), the 7th month of China (8 Aug. – 7 Sept.), and the 11th month of China (7 Dec 22 – 5 Jan 23). The month in which the financial slump and you need to be careful of unexpected expenses are: the second month, China (6 Jul. – 4 Apr.), 5th month of China (6 Jun. – 6 Jul.), 6th month of China (7 Jul. – 7 Aug.) and 8th month of China (8 Jul. – 7 Oct.) Allow others to borrow money and guarantee guarantees. Be mindful and avoid greed. Avoid gambling on various matters.

Family

Despite some disruptions, your family's destiny this year was guided by auspicious stars. However, the favorable stars will aid in the transformation of the heavy matter into lightness. This year, your home has set criteria for hosting an auspicious event. You will have the opportunity to add expensive assets to your home, or you may be able to relocate to a new residence, whether at your current address or work, or you may meet the criteria to add more new members to your family. However, if you enter the following month, you should be cautious of the chaos that occurs in the house.

including the 2nd month of China (6 Mar - 4 Apr), the 5th month of China (6 Jun - 6 Jul)., the 6th month of China (7 Jul. - 7 Aug.), and 8th month of China (8 Sep. - 7 Oct.) to be cautious of minors or servants causing problems while at work or traveling. You must exercise extreme caution to avoid mishaps. Also, be aware that family members' conflicts and sufferings can cause chaos in the family.

Love

The love story of destiny is the year that the relationship is smooth this year. You can use this opportunity to take your partner on a trip to distant lands or to contribute more than half of your life to making merit. You understand how to put If you can learn to let go and not make a big deal out of your children and grandchildren in this life, you will know what it means to be truly happy. But during the 2nd month of China (6 Mar. – 4 Apr.), the 5th month of China (6 Jun. – 6 Jul.), the 6th month of China (7 Jul. – 7 Aug.) and the 8th month of China (8 Sep. – 7 Oct.) You should avoid interfering with other people's families. Be wary that word-of-mouth can lead to conflict, and avoid going to entertainment venues because, in addition to bringing problems, they may also be infected with the disease.

Health

This year's physical health is not to be underestimated. Aside from the accumulated stress that causes you to sleep frequently, you should also be cautious of hepatitis, diabetes, high blood pressure, and diseases that cause joint and body aches. Especially during the month that destiny should pay more attention to health care, such as the 2nd month of China (6 March - 4 April), the 5th month of China (6 June - 6 July), the 6th month of China (7 July – 7 Aug) and the 8th month of China (8 Sept. – 7 Oct.) because there will be a lot of fire during this time. It is an opportunity for illnesses to request. To assist with this, find time to do some light exercise, such as swinging your arms forward and back or practicing qigong walking for 15 minutes three days a week or more. Even better, drink more than six glasses of warm, clean water per day. It will aid in the prevention of heat poisoning.

Year of the Rat (Water) | (1972)

" The Rat in the field" is a person born in the year of the Rat at the age of 51 years (1972)

Overview

There were various irregularities for those born in the year of the rat, around this age, because the year of his birth received a certain amount of power against Chong, falling into the "Phua" principle, as well as having a group of bad stars that orbited to cause a lot of trouble. Although there is a steady inflow of income from financial matters. However, there will be unexpected expenses that will require money from pocket. The commercial work will be challenging to complete. There are frequently factors that impede the slow progress of the work, including both colleagues and funds. Concerning family matters, there will be a reason for you to lose money to improve and repair equipment. If it is too heavy, it may be necessary to repair the house. Also this year, fate should be wary of children or servants in the house causing problems. Including valuable assets that are vulnerable to lose or theft. You should not be complacent about your health. You should find an opportunity to honor the gods and pray for blessings at the start of the year. Paying homage to the god Tai to avoid disaster will help to alleviate bad things.

Career and Business

This year's destiny business prompted him to work more due to a large number of expenses awaiting. However, it is believed that the additional funds invested this year will not be wasted. Because it will receive auspicious power to promote you in work, it will encourage you to do more, resulting in sales or visible work. Especially during the months when work and trade showed remarkable progress, namely the 12th month of China (5 Jan. – 3 Feb.), the 3rd month of China (5 Apr. – 5 May), the 7th month of China (8 Aug. – 7 Sep.) and 11th month of China (7 Dec. 22 – 5 Jan. 23), but if stepping into the 2nd month of China (6 Mar – 4 Apr), the 5th month of China (6 Jun - 6 Jul), the 6th month of China (7 Jul - 7 Aug) and the 8th month of China (8 Sep - 7 Oct.)

You should be aware that tax or accounting issues will cause complications. When signing contract documents, read the details thoroughly. Don't be fooled into being selfish until the lack of inspection causes you problems. Furthermore, be wary of negligent servants who cause damage, resulting in your liability.

Financial

The fortune teller's fortune this year may not be related to the job horoscope. Due to the large expenditures that are expected in the coming months, you must be diligent in rolling your money. Avoid gambling, gambling, or risk doing business that is illegal. Especially during the months that do not support you, such as the

2nd month of Chinese (6 Mar. – 4 Apr.), the 5th month of Chinese (6 Jun. – 6 Jul.), the 6th month of Chinese (7 Jul. – 7 Aug.) and the 8th month of China (8 Sept. – 7 Oct.), Do not wear decorations or place a temptation, including valuables, because they have the potential to be lost or stolen by thieves. For the months with the good financial flow, namely, the 12th month of China (5 Jan. – 3 Feb.), the 3rd month of China (5 Apr. – 5 May), the 7th month of China (8 Aug. – 7 Sep.) and 11th month of China (7 Dec. 22 – 5 Jan. 23).

Family

There are some positive aspects to destiny's family, but there are also some negative aspects. Because an auspicious event will occur in your home this year. This includes relocating to a new place of employment. More new members or engagements, baptisms, and family weddings are on the way. However, it will cause you to be concerned.

Especially during the bad months: 2nd month of China (6 Mar.- 4 Apr.), 5th month of China (6 Jun.- 6 Jul.), 6th month of China (7 Jul. – 7 Aug.), and the 8th month of China (8 Sep. – 7 Oct.)

where the family's fortunes are not rosy The fate must draw his attention to the safety of his family members. Be wary of mishaps that could result in injuries to people in the house. Be wary of disagreements with family members as well.

Love
Your love affairs are quite feudal this year. Even minor events can spark heated debate. If you both stand firm in your convictions without bending your elbows. There is a chance that the rupture will become much larger. As a result, it must be asked not to let him down. You're willing to compromise when you can't change the other side. There will be no narrative. During this sensitive month and ask you to support your love as much as 2nd month of Chinese (6 Mar. – 4 Apr.), 5th month of Chinese (6 Jun. – 6 Jul.), 6th month of China (7 Jul - 7 Aug) and the 8th month of China (8 Sep. - 7 Oct), When the incident is not satisfied and begins to argue, request that you leave. Let's talk again after you've calmed down in another corner. Furthermore, do not interfere with other people's families and avoid going to places of

entertainment because it will bring misery and trouble.

Health

This year, destiny has a criterion to get sick easily, especially the 2nd month of China (6 Mar. - 4 Apr.), 5th month of China (6 Jun. - 6 Jul.), 6th month of China (7 Jul. – 7 Aug.) and the 8th month of China (8 Sep. – 7 Oct.) As a result, you should practice good living hygiene. Eat well and keep an eye out for gastrointestinal diseases like gastritis, infectious diseases, allergies, and insomnia. You should be cautious of accidents that cause injuries while traveling this year, both near and far. You should also get adequate rest. Do not overburden yourself with work; let some go. Both should schedule vacation time with loved ones or family. Because, in addition to resting, it helps to promote family relationships in another way, and should make time to exercise regularly. Abuse of any kind, whether of alcohol or cigarettes, should be avoided.

Year of the Rat (Wood) | (1984)

" The rat in the mountains" is a person born in the year of the Rat at the age of 39 years (1984)

Overview

An auspicious star "Tian Ik" will be orbiting to help those born in the year of the rat, around this age, this year, even in the house of fate. However, you are unable to resist the influence of the "Phao," which causes your financial situation to be less than ideal. There will be a lot of turnover income even at the beginning and end of the year. However, when the money flowed out, the sum of money appeared to vanish instantly. As a result, working capital should be carefully managed during this critical year. This year may have to have a distance rhythm with friends and relatives. Because you will discover a type of sweet mouth, but there are other hidden purposes, so please be cautious not to be greedy Another thing to remember this year is that you should not lend money to anyone or sign a guarantee for someone else. Because the threshold for love and lover is high, be more cautious with words and disagreements. As a result, they must be calm and rational when conversing with one another. Because you belong to one of the zodiac signs. As a result, at the start of the year, you should find a way to pay homage to the god Tai so that all obstacles are removed.

Career and Business

The power of auspicious stars shining brightly has given this year's work a prosperous direction. In the middle to end of the year, job duties and trade will face some challenges. You will, however, be able to overcome obstacles. Please continue to be diligent and determined. It will lead to success. This year, you have the opportunity to change jobs or shift your responsibilities in a better direction.

Including the smooth and flexible trading, including the 12th month of China (5 Jan. – 3 Feb.), the 3rd month of China (5 Apr. – 5 May), the 7th month of China (8 Aug. – 7 Sep.), and the 11th month of China (7 Dec. 22 – 5 Jan. 23), but if entering the 2nd month of China (6 Mar. – 4 Apr.), 5th month of China (6 Jun - 6 Jul), 6th month of China (7 Jul - 7 Aug) and 8th month of China (8 Sep - 7 Oct), You should be cautious of the issue. Concerning the contract documents that will cause future harm as a result, various documents must be reviewed before signing the contract. Should pay close attention to the complexities.

Financial

In terms of fortune and money this year, you should consider the surrounding factors and make the best decision. Don't be solely selfish. Because decisions will have long-term consequences. Beautiful when there is a steady stream of income coming in. You must carefully allocate your investment and working capital. Both should follow the saving and saving principle. Because it appeared in front of it the expenditures awaiting not less than you should be cautious with your spending during this month of bad luck, namely, 2nd month of China (6 Mar. - 4 Apr.), 5th month of China (6 Jun. - 6 Jul.), 6th month of China. (7 Jul – 7 Aug.) and the 8th month of China (8 Sep. – 7 Oct.) Furthermore, you should not lend money to others or guarantee guarantees on their behalf. Don't be too greedy, and stay away from illegal activities. For months with a positive cash flow, namely, the 12th month of China (5 Jan. – 3 Feb.), the 3rd month of China (5 Apr. – 5 May), the 7th month of China (8 Aug. – 7 Sep.) and 11th month of China (7 Dec. 22 – 5 Jan. 23).

Family

The family's fortunes are fair this year. Even in the house, there will be good news and possibly auspicious events. Whether you are decorating, renovating, moving, painting, or saving for a new house. Including a variety of auspicious events such as an engagement, wedding, or the addition of new members. However, because your destiny has been afflicted with some evil powers, fate should be cautious about the safety of the elderly and children in the home. Avoid unintentional falls that cost you money and send you to the hospital. Furthermore, one must be cautious of minors who cause chaos and make the house unstable. The months that you need to add extra attention to are: the 2nd month of China (6 Mar. – 4 Apr.), 5th month of China (6 Jun. – 6 Jul.), 6th month of China (7 Jul. – 7 Aug.), and the 8th month of China (8 Sep. – 7 Oct.).

Love

The love of your destiny at the start of the good year, and the end of the bad year, so please be cautious of emotions that are easily irritated. The unconscious use of emotions causes some behavior, and speech, and may hurt the heart of the lover and lover until it accumulates. Sometimes the heartache has accumulated to the point of resentment, causing the event to spread widely. You need to be very careful, especially during the following months: the 2nd month of China (6 Mar. - 4 Apr.), the 5th month of China (6 Jun. - 6 Jul.), 6th month of China. (7 Jul - 7 Aug) and the 8th month of China (8 Sep - 7 Oct).

You should be cautious about becoming involved with other people's families because it can lead to arguments about a worthy life. Avoid going to places of entertainment. As a bonus, you may become ill.

Health

This year, destiny's general health is in good shape; there are no serious illnesses on the horizon, but there may be some airborne diseases, a cold, and nasal congestion. Please see a doctor as soon as possible and take medication to recover. Don't let it become chronic; there will be other complications, especially during the months when the destiny should add extra health care, such as the 2nd month of China (6 Mar. - 4 Apr.), the 5th month of China (6 Jun - 6 Jul), the 6th month of China (7 Jul. - 7 Aug.) and the 8th month of China (8 Sep. - 7 Oct.) If you drink alcohol or Drunken Pickles and have to work with tools - machines, use them carefully, be aware of dangers, and avoid car accidents.

Chinese Astrology Horoscope for Each Month

Month 12 in the Tiger Year (6 Jan 23 - 3 Feb 23)
The beginning of a new month is an auspicious occasion for destiny to meet his patron. The major events that have worried you over the last year will change more positively and smoothly this month. People will reach out to

assist you in finding a way out. As a result, whether it is financial or commercial. Everyone will find a way to make good progress.

This trade work period has been uneventful. As a result, you should use this opportunity to assess your weaknesses and find ways to apply them to your vision. It is critical to keep learning new things. Stay informed and learn new technologies to prepare for your opponents' next round of challenges.

This salary, even if you have a lot of income, will have a lot of expenses, so you must try to reduce all unnecessary expenses to maintain liquidity and have leftovers.

You will receive good news from your family as a result of the auspicious stars orbiting the zodiac house. It is about the progress of the members of the house.

Relatives and friends who are stuck in any situation will be helped.

No disease persecution for the benefit of health

The love aspect is regarded as pleasant. You have the opportunity to travel long distances together to fill the honey of love and impress them. However, investments in various fields If you can avoid it during this month, you should. because they have the right to be exhausted, liberated, and squandered.

Support Days: 2 Jan., 6 Jan., 10 Jan., 14 Jan., 18 Jan., 22 Jan., 26 Jan., 30 Jan.
Lucky Days: 7 Jan., 19 Jan., 31 Jan.
Misfortune Days: 12 Jan., 24 Jan.
Bad Days: 1 Jan, 3 Jan, 13 Jan, 15 Jan, 25 Jan., 27 Jan.

Month 1 in the Rabbit Year (4 Feb 23 - 5 Mar 23)
Your destiny as a rat born in the year of the rat, even if it falls in the first year of the year, is the principle of "Phua," but you do not have to be afraid if you have strong willpower and stand firm in your carelessness. If you have time at the beginning of the year, you should go to pay

homage to the god Tai to discourage and dispel danger. Because your horoscope for this month is not favorable. There are still thorny issues to consider in terms of work and trade. As a result, each activity should be planned. and allocate wise spending from the start of the year It's better than waiting for an incident to occur and then showing up to deal with it when it's too late. Furthermore, they should not interfere with or interfere with the responsibilities of others.

The financial horoscope is below average. However, you should spend your money wisely and make investments in various areas before giving up gambling and gambling. Avoid lending money or providing guarantees to anyone.

The family is at peace, but be wary of strangers visiting the house to trick you into losing your property during this time. You will not lose if you do not become greedy.

The body's health is deteriorating. Be wary of recurring diseases and hidden diseases. You should always take care of the elderly's eating and living hygiene in the house, keeping it clean and paying close attention. Be wary of mishaps.

Those who are single and unmarried will have the opportunity to meet the right person soon.

Support Days: 3 Feb., 7 Feb., 11 Feb., 15 Feb., 19 Feb.   23 Feb., 27 Feb.
Lucky Days: 12 Feb., 24 Feb.
Misfortune Days: 5 Feb., 17 Feb.
Bad Days: 6 Feb., 8 Feb., 18 Feb., 20 Feb.

Month 2 in the Rabbit Year (6 Mar 23 - 5 Apr 23)
This month's horoscope is even better than the previous month's. However, the road was still cloudy. Be wary of unforeseen obstacles in the workplace, including the business of destiny. What you should do this month is that if you are complacent about a problem for an extended time, it will grow into a large problem that will be difficult to solve later. Both must exercise

extreme caution when dealing with a wide range of working relationships. and always keeping the goals in mind.

If you are unhappy, you may have to turn the money in a spiral left hand and pay out the right hand, and if you have outstanding sales, you should follow up before the due date because if you are unhappy, there may be more bad debt accounts.

For the sake of peace family, Parents and children relied on each other to provide love and encouragement.

In general, relatives and friends will be helped and supported. However, if you talk too much, it can easily turn into negative speech, causing conflicts to avoid looking at each other.

When it comes to your health, you must be especially cautious and take care of yourself. Not getting enough sleep in particular. Furthermore, eating fatty foods will aggravate other diseases. You should also drink more water this month because you will be more influenced by the Fire element than usual.

The love story is ordinary. There will be no cause for rupture if you continue to stir the water or bring up old stories.

For those looking for new investment opportunities. During this time, there is a bright future that can be realized. There will be sufficient profit for you to reap.

Support Days: 3 Mar., 7 Mar., 11 Mar., 15 Mar., 19 Mar., 23 Mar., 27 Mar., 31 Mar.
Lucky Days: 8 Mar., 20 Mar.
Misfortune Days: 1 Mar., 13 Mar., 25 Mar.
Bad Days: 2 Mar., 4 Mar., 14 Mar., 16 Mar., 26 Mar., 28 Mar.

Month 3 in the Rabbit Year (6 Apr 23 - 5 May 23)
This month marks the beginning of the partner month for those born in the year of the rat. It is like the sky after the rain that appears with rainbows at the end of the sky, in addition to receiving auspicious energy from the good

stars. All financial matters have been granted auspicious power to visit. So you should increase your diligence and determination. Can't rely on one job; must find a way to increase revenue to increase sales.

This salary horoscope has a plentiful income stream. However, because there are numerous income channels, even with a large income, expenses can catch up with the shadows. As a result, you should set aside some reserves so that there is liquidity available during times of congestion. Some come in for the fortune. However, you should not put in too much effort. will result in more losses than gains.

Peace and harmony are beneficial to the family.

Although there were some disagreements in love, they were minor. It is natural for tongues and teeth to rub against each other.

excellent relatives There will be an adult on hand to provide guidance. To receive assistance, you must be stuck on any issue.

Work and investments during this period are sufficient, but before making any decisions. To avoid future conflicts, discussions, and details should be documented before taking action.

Support Days: 4 Apr., 8 Apr., 12 Apr., 16 Apr., 20 Apr., 24 Apr., 28 Apr.
Lucky Days: 1 Apr., 13 Apr., 25 Apr.
Misfortune Days: 6 Apr., 18 Apr., 30 Apr.
Bad Days: 7 Apr., 9 Apr., 19 Apr., 21 Apr.

Month 4 in the Rabbit Year (6 May 23 - 5 Jun 23)
In the aftermath of the previous month's chaos, this month's fate criterion has not yet been concluded. Financial and employment issues There are still old stories circulating that you must fix and continue to spread. During this time, you should focus on resolving any outstanding issues. Use your previous mistakes as teachers to devise a new game-changing move.

The salary is reasonable. However, you must continue to follow the previous measures to save money on seat belts. because it appears that unexpected small expenses will drain money from the pocket If you are not careful with your spending, you have the right to have a dry face at the end of the month as well.

Even during this period, you will be in a state of flux in terms of work, including business affairs. However, you will be able to find new avenues for future trade directions if you are fortunate enough to find supporters.

The family is currently at peace, with no cause for contention. However, health is important; avoid getting sick or having allergy problems. Nasal congestion, body aches, headaches, and insomnia are common symptoms.

It is the season of love when the love tree blooms and bears fruit. A warm and sweet relationship exists. This rhythm is a good time to achieve fulfillment for those who want to confess their feelings to their loved ones but are still afraid.

Investing in various fields is possible, but the results are not very promising. However, there will be no loss after falling.

Support Days: 2 May., 6 May., 10 May., 14 May., 18 May., 22 May., 26 May., 26 May.
Lucky Days: 7 May., 9 May., and 31 May.
Misfortune Days: 12 May., 24 May.
Bad Days: 1 May., 3 May., 13 May., 15 May., 25 May., 27 May.

Month 5 in the Rabbit Year (6 Jun 23 - 6 Jul 23)

This month's journey through life saw many evil stars interfering with orbiting. Many of the things he intends to cling to are uncertain, especially the unexpected. As a result, not only should life be more careful and knowledgeable in terms of planning and operations. This month, here's what you should do. Take care of your workload as best you can, and don't interfere or interfere with the work of others. It is also critical that you do not attend the funeral service this month.

Lose the seat for money, even if the income is good because unexpected expenses will suck money out, causing a lack of liquidity. As a result, all forms of gambling are prohibited. And don't be overly greedy in your pursuit of riches through illegal business.

There are frequent conflicts between upper and lower levels of management in this stage of work and business. As a result, I ask that you exercise good emotional control. The signing of various contract documents during this time should be scrutinized more closely.

During this time, keep an eye on the health of the elderly in the house. And should closely monitor the safety of household members, as the stellar group that is being targeted during this period has criteria that may be mourning for an adult relative.

Be wary of changes in this love horoscope. They may have to spend more time together.

This is not the time to start a new job or make investments in various fields.

Support Days: 3 Jun., 7 Jun., 11 Jun., 15 Jun., 19 Jun., 23 Jun., 27 Jun.
Lucky Days: 12 Jun., 24 Jun.
Misfortune Days: 5 Jun., 17 Jun., 29 Jun.
Bad Days: 6 Jun., 8 Jun., 18 Jun., 20 Jun., 30 Jun.

Month 6 in the Rabbit Year (7 Jul 23 - 7 Aug 23)

This month, your fate is not beyond the monsoon line. Furthermore, many evil stars specialize in harassment. Even though the overall job and business environment is improving. However, there is still the issue of the person's constant turbulence. In such a situation, it is easy for a minor issue to escalate into a major one. As a result, please do your best to mitigate the damage. Rituals may be necessary at times to help build morale and morale. Making merit and making merit together will aid in the relief of bleeding and the avoidance of danger.

There is still a story for you to pay attention to regarding the horoscope. There is a high risk associated with fortune money. So, instead of getting your hopes up, cut back on unnecessary extravagant spending. Take care that liquidity does not get stuck in front of you rather than behind you.

This month's family horoscope was misplaced. You will need to be more cautious to keep your valuables safe. Be wary of thieves, especially those who bring salt into the house. And should be cautious of accidents that may occur to members of the household. Sharp objects or objects with the potential to cause hazards and flammability must be formally inspected and stored.

Avoid visiting entertainment venues during this period of love to avoid problems from third parties. Which will cause issues for the family

The health is fine, but you should avoid having an affair after drinking.

Investing during this time should be avoided.

Support Days: 1 Jul., 5 Jul., 9 Jul., 13 Jul., 17 Jul., 21 Jul., 25 Jul., 29 Jul.
Lucky Days: 6 Jul., 18 Jul., 30 Jul.
Misfortune Days: 11 Jul., 23 Jul.
Bad Days: 2 Jul., 12 Jul., 14 Jul., 24 Jul., 26 Jul.

Month 7 in the Rabbit Year (8 Aug 23 - 7 Sep 23)
The fate criterion for this month has passed through the monsoon season and entered alliance territory. There are also fortunate stars that shine brightly above the zodiac fate. Work and business functions have found a way forward as a result. This is an excellent opportunity to build a portfolio or increase sales of your planned plans and funds. Let's make the most of it this month. It will have the ability to propel it very far.

This aspect of pay is abundant. Income is coming in from a variety of sources. You have the right to win money in your pocket if you gamble, hoping for a floating fortune or stock lottery.

This is a peaceful time in the family. The house has a bright atmosphere. The members who are loving and reconciling are cheerful and full of smiles. When the energy inside the house is smooth, work outside the home benefits as well.

This is a powerful time in the health horoscope. Those who have congenital or chronic diseases during this time will be able to see a good doctor to help treat their symptoms.

In memory of those who are still unmarried. The relationship will move forward smoothly. However, those who have a partner or partner should exercise caution when using words that could lead to an argument. and should refuse friends who invite them to entertainment venues because it will cause them endless problems.

According to the horoscope, relatives and friends will have criteria for merit-making, charity work, or social contribution activities together in various investments during this period. The green light will flower and fruit for a long time during this period.

Support Days: 2 Aug., 6 Aug., 10 Aug., 14 Aug., 18 Aug., 22 Aug., 26 Aug., 30 Aug.
Lucky Days: 11 Aug., 23 Aug.
Misfortune Days: 4 Aug., 16 Aug., 28 Aug.
Bad Days: 5 Aug., 7 Aug., 17 Aug., 19 Aug., 29 Aug., 31 Aug.

Month 8 in the Rabbit Year (8 Sep 23 - 7 Oct 23)

Your fate criterion This month has a high concentration of evil stars clinging to the group. As a result, life during this time is frequently stalled, with problems and disruptions. During this time, you should be wary of the cause that will result in a slew of lawsuits. Copyright should be considered when using product images or text. Accounting taxes must also be properly prepared. They should also be cautious of conflicts, contract breaches, and fines under various conditions.

During this time, if there is any story, you should tell it. Please keep your distance and avoid using harsh words or challenging behaviors. It will aid in the reduction.

Money is an issue this month, with a low income and an overwhelming expenditure. Saving money and finding new ways to make money will help you solve the problem. Gambling, fortune, bad luck, stock lottery investing, and speculation in various fields Should avoid investing in high-risk businesses and lending money to others. including the execution of numerous guarantee contracts

There are frequent disagreements within the family. Maintaining the hope of winning with the people in the house is not the solution, and do not disregard the safety of the people in the house.

During this time, you should make time to meditate and let go of your physical and mental health.

This month, relatives and friends may have to distance themselves because of problems that will not bother you. Love remains stable. Although there are some emotional conflicts. However, it is not a major issue. Use the road if you are traveling by car during this time. Take no chances.

Support Days: 3 Sep, 7 Sep., 11 Sep, 15 Sep, 19 Sep., 23 Sep. 27 Sep.
Lucky Days: 4 Sep., 16 Sep., 28 Sep.
Misfortune Days: 9 Sep., 21 Sep.
Bad Days: 10 Sep., 12 Sep., 22 Sep., 24 Sep.

Month 9 in the Rabbit Year (8 Oct 23 - 6 Nov 23)
This month's destiny will be more prosperous. It is an excellent opportunity for those who are trading or working full-time, as well as those who are considering investing in various fields.

because there is still a workable response What you should do when there are many opportunities and options, including money, and beautiful numbers that rise at this time. To make your investment worthwhile, you should be cautious and thorough. Don't be greedy in every way because the average outcome isn't worth it.

When income is fixed, this salary horoscope is mediocre. As a result, it should not add to the burden on oneself and one's family. Using money to gamble with luck, can only result in irreversible losses.

In terms of work, you must carefully consider any work activities, including signing contract documents, during this period. Impatient people cause harm and do not provide guarantees for others. In terms of starting a new job or investing. During this time, there is a bright direction. Can be expanded both internally and externally will have a chance to earn good returns

There are no serious illnesses to be concerned about in terms of health.

Relatives and friends should be cautious of your actions and words. When discussing anything, keep the other person in mind. It can have an impact on your relationship if you are not careful.

In this affection, The more emotionally charged things become, the more arguments there are. Little things have a way of becoming big things. You'll need to be patient. Excessive stretching will cause the girl's length to be increased.

Support Days: 1 Oct., 5 Oct., 9 Oct., 13 Oct., 17 Oct., 21 Oct., 25 Oct., 29 Oct.
Lucky Days: 10 Oct., 22 Oct.
Misfortune Days: 3 Oct., 15 Oct., 27 Oct.
Bad Days: 4 Oct., 6 Oct., 16 Oct., 18 Oct., 28 Oct., 30 Oct.

Month 10 in the Rabbit Year (7 Nov 23 - 6 Dec 23)
This month, your life path has returned to confront the crisis with an unlucky star that orbits to aim in the position. As a result, the fate is to be cautious of accidents both during travel and at work. Be wary of the risk of bleeding when using tools. And it's another month when people tend to grieve for respected elders.

In terms of trade, there are risks associated with volatile events that are difficult to predict. and should avoid being slandered or accused until the obstacles obstruct progress in the work.

The only thing that can help is emotional control. A pleasant conversation shows consideration for others. This will aid in the reduction of problems and bullying.

On the plus side, this salary is reasonable. There is a consistent flow of revenue. However, expenditures are being closely monitored. As a result, it is critical to plan your spending and always save money so that you do not need it in an emergency.

During this time, you should be cautious of heart disease, internal swelling, and food poisoning. and other hidden diseases that will indicate that he will appear, including traveling both near and far in this distance Safety should be prioritized.

There will be frequent clashing problems in a love that is not smooth.

This month is not ideal for starting a new job and investing. should be avoided before being considered safe.

Support Days: 2 Nov., 6 Nov., 10 Nov., 14 Nov., 18 Nov., 22 Nov., 26 Nov., 30 Nov.
Lucky Days: 3 Nov., 15 Nov., 27 Nov.
Misfortune Days: 8 Nov., 20 Nov.
Bad Days: 9 Nov., 11 Nov., 21 Nov., 23 Nov.

Month 11 in the Rabbit Year (7 Dec 23 - 5 Jan 24)

This month, your destiny has been turned upside down and met with light. Tian Ik and Tribute Ha, who orbited to visit, were influenced by the auspicious stars. As a result, job duties, including trade, will improve. Obstacles and problems were overcome, and there are people available to provide advice to help the work run smoothly again. Those who work full-time or serve in the government this month will recognize the significance. As a result, I request that you do your best to complete the assigned tasks. Don't be discouraged if the work is difficult.

This financial fortune is still sufficient to provide income from pocket. Think, hope, gamble, speculate, and you will be wealthy if you smell good. However, one should not be overly greedy because there are still unforeseen expenses to contend with.

Events within the family can relieve tensions and provide good news about the addition of new members or the success of the people in the home. You both have the fortune to move and move. It could be relocating to a new home or relocating to a new job. or you must travel to distant lands for work.

Physically, I was in good shape. Be wary of diseases that will arise as a result of indulgences and food poisoning during this time.

Relatives and friends gathered to assist and have the opportunity to work together in trading joint ventures.

It's a perfect time for some people to fall in love. It's a good time for a second or third round of engagement, wedding, or honeymoon travel.

Support Days: 4 Dec., 8 Dec., 12 Dec., 16 Dec., 20 Dec., 24 Dec., 28 Dec.
Lucky Days: 9 Dec., 21 Dec.
Misfortune Days: 2 Dec., 14 Dec., 26 Dec.
Bad Days: 3 Dec., 5 Dec., 15 Dec., 17 Dec., 27 Dec., 29 Dec.

Amulet for The Year of the Rat
"The God Cheng Dao Zhou"

This year, those born in the year of the rat should establish and worship sacred objects. "The God Cheng Dao Zhou" to improve fortune by placing it on the desk or cash desk to request the power of his prestige to assist in protecting the destiny from all dangers that result from The unfortunate stars that will collide this year will be destroyed, but only in a good way.

Throughout the year, fortune and wealth are abundant.

(Note: The final text of your life cycle can be used to determine the direction in which sacred objects should be established.)

Chapter one of the Department of Advanced Feng Shui discusses the gods who will descend to reside in the yearly mikeng (destiny house), who are the gods who can bring both good and bad to the fate of that year. When this occurs, the worship is supplemented by gods who come down to reside regularly in the year of your birth. As a result, it is thought to produce the best results and has the greatest impact on you. Misfortunes will be alleviated to rely on the majesty of the gods to protect him while his destiny is in decline, while also asking for your blessings to help inspire smooth business activities as you desire. Bring you and your family luck and prosperity.

Those born in the year of the rat or Mi Keng (destiny house) are under the sign of the rat.

Many auspicious stars are shining brightly this year. Work and commerce are thus powerful. It's been a year full of possibilities. Everything will be fine if everything is well planned. However, there is a star destroyer in fate. Furthermore, his birth year falls on the "Phua" digit, making it the year of their union. As a result, be wary of job and financial turnaround events that peak in the first half of the year and decline in the second. Be wary of being duped or robbed at the end of the year, which could result in injury. They must avoid being greedy and greedy. Senior ladies in love, beware of losing money in September. The single man will meet with friends to take care of his life. Those who are married should not be considerate of others. Otherwise, the marriage will undoubtedly fail. If you want to solve your misfortune and improve your destiny, you should make and wear amulets. "The God Cheng Dao Zhou" to request the power of his prestige to aid in the abolition of disasters. Fixed the killing power of the evil star. Aids in the promotion of destiny's work and business to prosper, progress, fortune, wealth, good health, and within the family to avoid safety and prosperity.

According to Taoist traditions, three gods are revered by a large number of people. The three gods are collectively referred to as "Sanqing," and their full name is "Sanqing." "San Qingjing Dong Shen Jiao Zhu," or "Three Wisdom Gods," is a high god with the highest maturity among the gods. They are ranked as follows:
1. "God Yan Zi Tianjun" (God Cheng Daozhou)
2. "Ling God Bao Tianjun," and
3. "God Tai Qing Dao De Tianjun" (God Tai Cheng Daozhou)

The primal deity is thought to be "God Cheng Dao Zhou." The first deity of all gods, waiting in eternity to teach the teachings of all beings. (Preliminary eternity), "Ling Bao Tianjun" preached the Dharma in the Middle Ages to teach all beings. (Early eternity) and "Thep Tai Cheng Tao Zhou" preaching and teaching the Dharma to these creatures in the last eternity. (For all eternity)

"God Cheng Dao Zhou" translates literally as "Great God of the Beginning" or "Lord of All Things." It is said that there was no sky, no earth, and no moon at the beginning of the universe.

In the void of the universe, the moon has no stars. "Monk Cheng Dao Zhou" was born in the center of the universe and has been meditating for four eons. (Because "one eternity" is equal to "forty-one billion years" in Taoist belief, he is a symbol of the cosmic power that gives birth to all things. Out of misfortune, sorrow, and no bully to find a convenient way in the business of various trades and help make everything smooth and full.

Those born in the year of the rat should also wear an auspicious pendant. "Thep Nghek Cheng Tao Zhou" around your neck or carry it with you when you go outside the house, both near and far. so that your destiny is blessed with abundant wealth Throughout the year, there is prosperity and progress in business, business, business, family peace, and happiness, resulting in good efficiency and effectiveness. faster than ever before.

Good Direction: Southeast, North, and Southwest
Bad Direction: South
Lucky Colors: Blue, Gray, Blue, White, Gold, and Silver
Lucky Times: 07.00 – 08.59, 15.00 – 16.59, 23.00 – 02.59.
Bad Times: 11.00 – 11.59, 13.00 – 14.59, 17.00 – 18.59.

Good Luck For 2023

CPSIA information can be obtained
at www.ICGtesting.com
Printed in the USA
LVHW102319130123
737118LV00001B/160